Artistic Intelligence
"How to unlock the artist within"

Published as a self-published author by Angelique Stefan, Los Angeles, CA.

1

Artistic Intelligence
"How to unlock the artist within"

For permission to use anything from this book or to get in contact with the publisher you can request through email at:

Rebellious.Spirit.59@gmail.com

Cover design: Designed by Angelique Stefan

Published in the United States of America

Artistic Intelligence

"How to unlock the artist within"

By

Angelique Stefan

Artistic Intelligence
"How to unlock the artist within"

Introduction

Artistic Intelligence
"How to unlock the artist within"

There are a lot of books that talk about shading. This book is here to teach you how to shade and blend only. Not many can master shading after still buying books. It is not easy teaching people how to draw, sketch or shade. The author reveals and exposes a short cut. No more reading for long hours on things you still can't understand. The author invented a grading scale formula to teach you how to master shading in less than half the time. All you must do is follow all her guidelines and exercises, and you too will be able to shade. This template she created will be the starting point of being able to finally master shading. She named the templet "The Miracle shading graph." You will learn some warmups, that will make it enough, to master what you intend to do.

Contents

Artistic Intelligence
"How to unlock the artist within"

Artistic Intelligence
"How to unlock the artist within"

Chapter 1 ....…..…… *Master of Art*
(Pages 13-18)
Chapter 2 ...... *Supplies and how they work*
(Pages 19-28)
Chapter 3 ……….…..... *Before the exercises*
(Pages 29-38)
Chapter 4 ……...............*The Miracle Graph*
(Pages 39-48)
Chapter 5 ……..... *Shadows and Highlights*
(Pages 49-64)
Chapter 6 ... *Preparation and transferring*
(Pages 65-72)
Chapter 7 ....…. *Put the shading to practice*
(Pages 73-84)
Chapter 8 ……..... *Review what you learned*
(Pages 85-92)

A message from the author
(Pages 93-98)

Acknowledgements
(Pages 99-104)

Artistic Intelligence
"How to unlock the artist within"

Chapter 1

"Master of Art"

Artistic Intelligence
"How to unlock the artist within"

Learning how to do shading for either portraits, objects or landscapes is much easier than you think! I will be teaching you how to master shading for anything that comes your way. All you need to do is master what I show you and you will see the changes in your work. There is no need to ramp on about useless amount of information and over talk when shading is much simpler. I would recommend drawing something first with the best of your ability to be able to use it and compare with future work. I

15

will also be showing you the pencils to use so that you can get the best quality in your contrast. This can really bring some income potential.

Can you picture your self-selling copies of the original work? If you answered to yourself "no or not yet," then you will see yourself differently by the end of this book. That answer will turn into a "definitely!" I mean none of this can go wrong. The average price for a big pack of blank paper goes between $0.99 cents to $10.00 depending on how many sheets you get. Hundreds of drawings can be created and duplicated for as many times as you'd like. The great part of this is, you won't spend too much just to make it happen. With the same materials you will be able to use it for more than a great number of sheets before you even run out.

Sky is the limit when selling and everything is all profit. This is when you realize that people pay for what is in the mind. Now, this book is only here to help you master shading. I will briefly explain other things like contrast, lighting, highlighting and helping you apply the shading to create a 3D fold. There will be discussions taking place about some of the items you can use to better assist you to create a greater look and bring out more potential. I invite you to try my methods without judgement. Don't be too

17

hard on yourself. Relax, take a deep breath and center yourself. Print 7 of the same black and white pictures of your choice. It must be a picture you can write over and ruin. Try to choose something that doesn't have too much complexity so that we can focus on showing you how to master the shading part first.

Chapter 2

"Supplies and how they work"

Artistic Intelligence
"How to unlock the artist within"

There are packs of small boxes at stores that carry pencils. Which one is right for the type of quality you want to produce? Well, there is never a right or wrong, it's just whatever works or doesn't work. This is just about the quality you are aiming for. There are many different boxes and brands. The main thing I would encourage is, find a box that carries different pencil grades or pencil scales. To make it easier, look at the top of the pencils and find the following

21

information; 8H, 7H, 6H, 5H, 4H, 3H, 2H, H, F, HB, B, 2B, 3B, 4B, 5B, 6B, 7B, 8B. Each pencil should have a number and a letter together. The type I just mentioned is called the HB scale or the HB graphite scale.

Now, there might be more to the scale that I did not mention, but this will get you through your intent. There are some boxes that carry half of the one's I mentioned. This is fine too. What I usually do is I get every other one just to keep things under budget and still get the results I am looking for. My favorite drawing pencils are "Staedtler Lumograph Drawing and Sketching" pencils. They should be at almost every

22

art store.

Now let me ask you this, have you ever come across any of the grades of these pencils? Maybe even just one? If the answer is "no," then think again. The number 2 pencil is what you have used your entire life including at school. It is really the HB in the scale. So, you do have some type of experience already, you were just not aware of it. You already know the harder you press, the darker it is on the paper, or the lighter your stroke, then the lighter it is on the paper. You see! You got it! It's just that the number 2 can be labeled differently when working with grading scale called the numerical graphite scale for pencils. Same thing worded different.

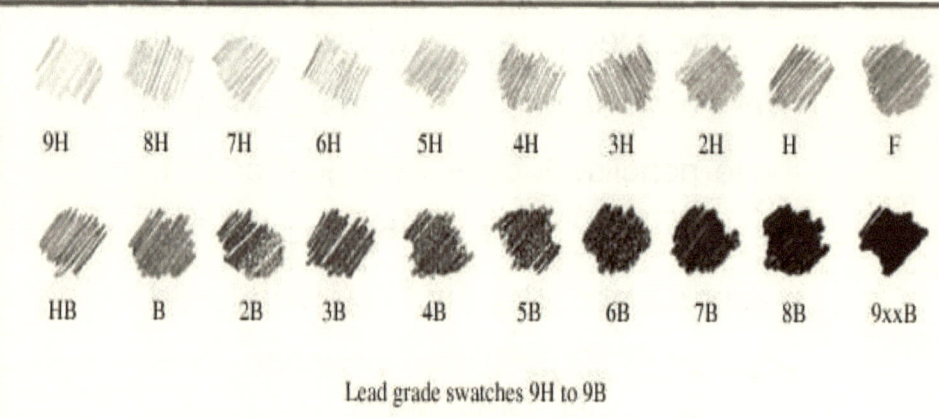

Lead grade swatches 9H to 9B

https://pencils.com/hb-graphite-grading-scale

Pencils explained

Here is a great reference I found that will help widen your mind on what each pencil can do as I continue to further explain. That way you start understanding the visual as you continue to read. The pencils that I usually get are HB, 6B, 4B, 2B, HB, 2H, 4H, 6H. They do have different box sets; it is up to you on what you feel. I recommend the same ones I use. Anywhere in-between you can blend and match. Let's get into detail about the pencils. The "H" stands for hard, which comes out light on paper. The higher in number that is next to the "H", then the lighter it is. The "B" stands for bold or black. The higher in number that is next to the "B" then the bolder and darker it is. The number 2 HB pencil is right in between it all. Just take a closer look at the scale image and you will see what each pencil is set to do.

Some other good tools to have while trying to get started are:

- Paper stumps (some are double ended)
- Trillion
- White eraser and a kneadable eraser (both)
- Stainless steel erasing shield
- Sandpaper pointer
- Artist tape
- Graphite paper (optional)
- Pencil sharpener
- Artist dusting brush (optional)
- Artist fixative clear coat spray (optional)

The supplies explained

The fixative clear coat spray is used to add a permanent protection to your artwork so that the pencil doesn't wear off and the quality stays. Try to spray this somewhere outside and wear a mask so that you do not breath those chemicals. The artist tape is great since it has less adhesive to protect your work from being damaged. You still must be careful even when pulling the tape. The dust brush is used to dust what you erase so that you do not use your hands and make a mistake that is hard to fix.

Drawing can be messy and wiping off the dust with your hands can lead to damage.

The stainless-steel erasing shield is great when you want to erase a very small portion. This shield can prevent you from erasing more than intended. The sandpaper pointer can help you sand off the over worked and dark left over from all the blending when using the paper stumps, to give it a fresh layer. The kneadable eraser is like a stretchy texture. It helps to lighten up the shading a bit in case you went too dark. You can dab the area you want to lighten.

Chapter 3

"Before the exercises"

Artistic Intelligence
"How to unlock the artist within"

There are specific things you need to learn and do before you can start or complete a drawing. One of the things I will explain is that each pencil is responsible for creating a different tone with-in the gradient scale. The exercise you are about to do, will help you memorize tones and practice hand strokes. This way when you approach your drawing, you will have a bigger idea of what to expect when trying to complete

Artistic Intelligence
"How to unlock the artist within"

it. Our hands and fingers tend to get stiff during the beginning stages of a drawing. Don't worry if you can't do it yet, this book will help you.

When you are sketching, it is important to allow your fingers to be light and flexible. Know when to add pressure and when to release pressure. This will allow your stroke to get lighter and less heavy or the opposite. This way you learn how to manipulate the pencil and you can create a dark to light effect. Try to draw a line with more pressure and as you start to move, get your hand pressure a little lighter. Get even more lighter as you go. This way you will see the dark to light affect. You can always try the same technique backwards where you go from light to dark just to loosen up your fingers. Dark to light curves will also help your hand and fingers to loosen up.

Okay, so now that you became familiar with that, I will show you the next step to prepare you for the actual warm up exercise. With art, the goal is to get the shading as smooth as possible. In realism, there is no inconsistency in the shading. Either the tone is solid and all a flat tone no matter what tone it is, or the shading goes from light to dark. So, grab a paper and any pencil you like. Then, draw a line that shows from dark to light. Now, here's where it gets tricky. I want you to copy that exact line right next to the one you just did. Don't leave any open gaps in between and match as much as you can with the same stroke and tone. Repeat this exercise for about 5 lines and you will see how this is starting to come together. This is all here to help you until you learn how to manipulate the pencils and some of the art supplies. I encourage you to utilize the paper stumps for shading. It can really help your shading to smoothen.

Another way to smoothen out the shading, especially when using the bold pencils is to use a pencil grade numbers with the "H" and sketch over it. This really helps shade very small missing spots that the previous bold pencils could not fill. For example, if "6B" looks patchy and wasn't able to cover very minor spots no matter how much you tried, then any "H" would cover it. It would help spread the "B" because the "B" is looser. This method is only used if you have already sharpened the pencils and still have not been able to get into some very small details.

Be very patient. The goal is quality. Take your time. Take as many breaks as you need. The more breaks you take, the more you can see what you need. This is because you gave your eyes and body a rest. The brain does get tired. Avoid creating dents as much as possible. You avoid this by drawing in layers. The more

35

layers you add without pressing hard, the smoother and darker you can make it look while taking your time. It is always better to build the look. If you do not see the tone you want, you can always go back and add another layer.

It is good to warm up and loosen up your fingers. There are some stroke practices that you can do to help better your shading. Once you learn the shading, then learning more art becomes a little easier. Understanding dark to light will really help take you to the next step in art. Especially when being able to master the quality you would like.

Cross hatch warmups:

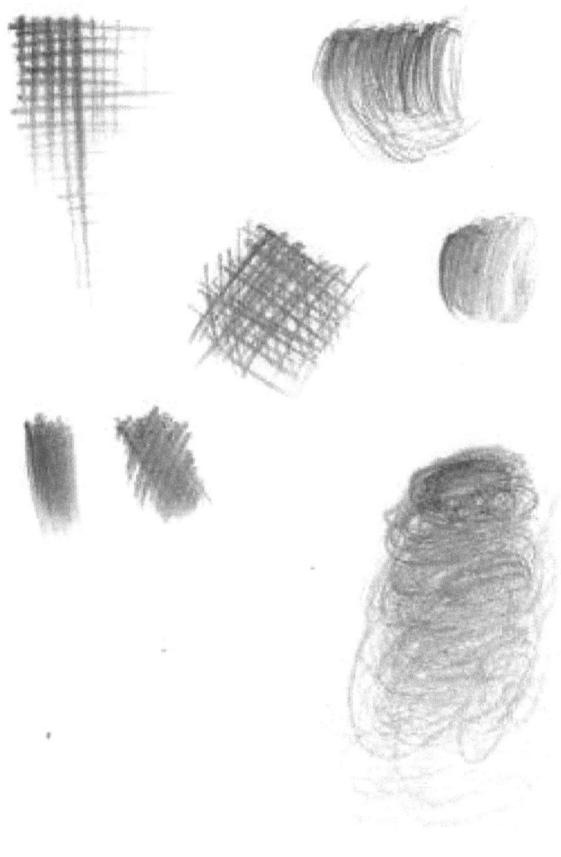

Artistic Intelligence
"How to unlock the artist within"

Chapter 4

"The miracle graph"

Artistic Intelligence
"How to unlock the artist within"

On a blank piece of paper, draw a couple circles. Try to draw at least 8 circles with a diameter of 1 ½ inches. Also add 2 rectangles. One that is 4-inch width by ½ inch height. The last rectangle would be 7-inch width by 1-inch height. What we will do now is write over the circle and add one pencil gradient each. It should look like this:

41

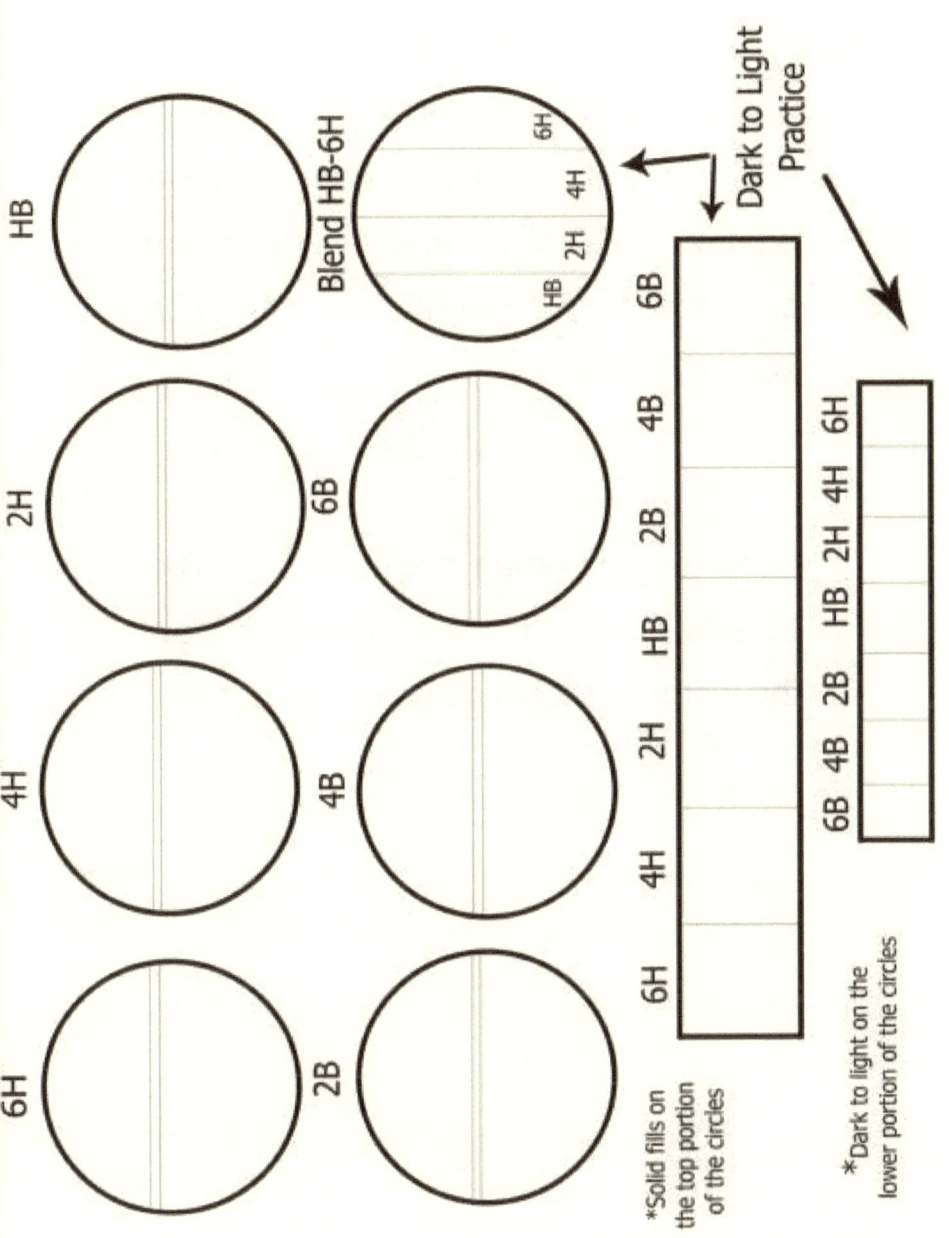

43

Towards the end of this book I attached a copy of a blank warm up sheet, so you can photocopy it instead. This way it can save you time.

I created this graph and named it "The Miracle Graph." Here is an idea of how the warmup should be completed:

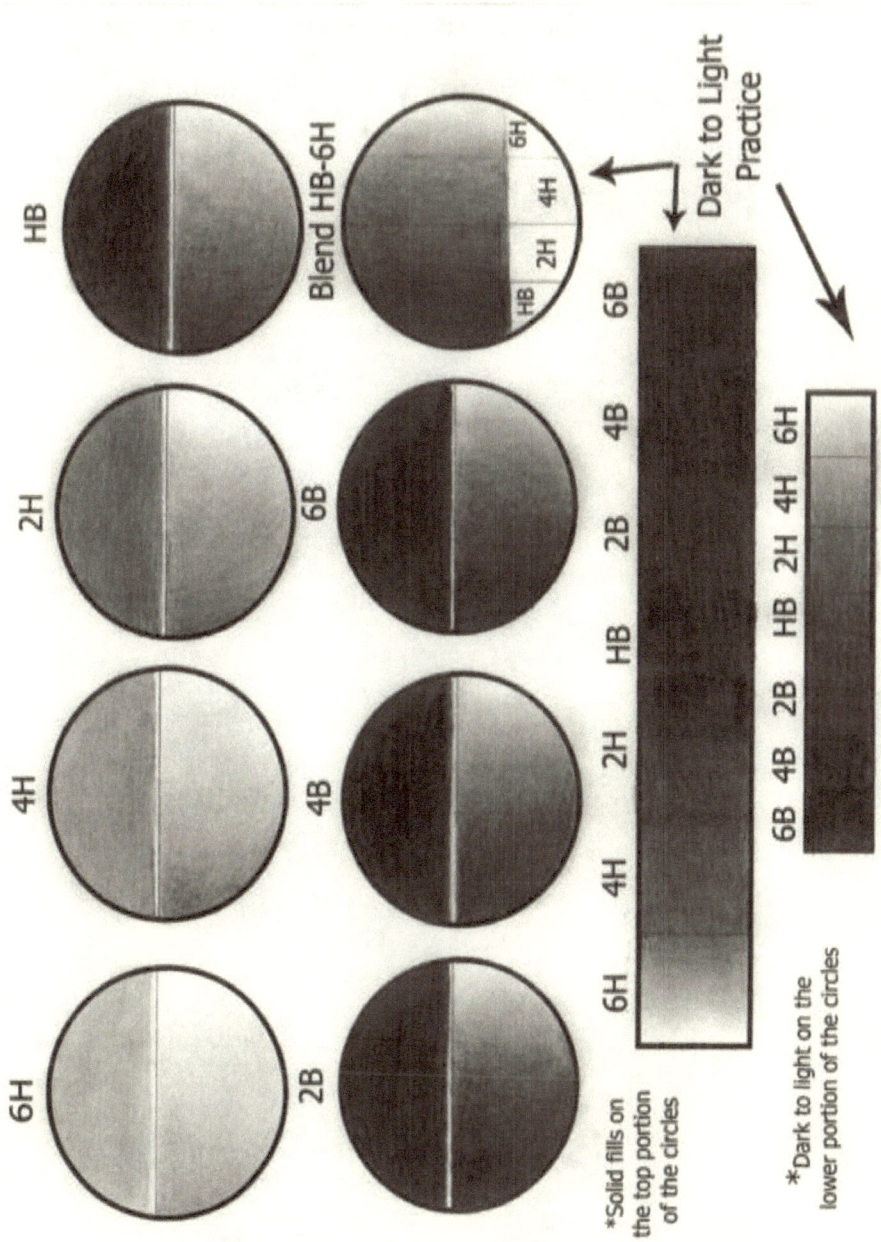

45

Avoid the Miracle graph warm-ups to look like this if you say it is your finished piece:

HB

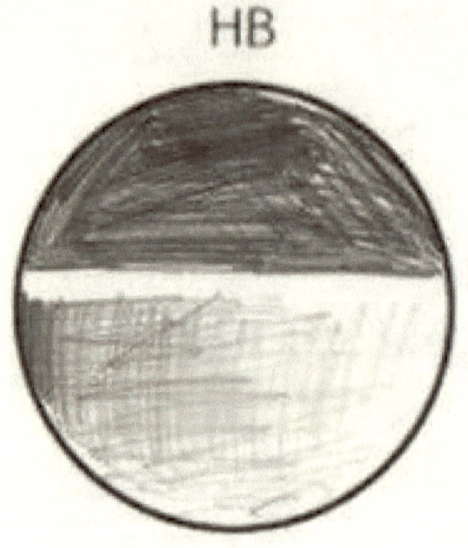

A good way to fix this if you are unsure, is first stop what you are doing. Then use the previous graph to remind you how to mimic that tone. You only pencil in the small empty hole areas and match it with the lines right around it. Then you can use the trillion or the paper stump to blend and smoothen it out. Try to use the paper stump or trillion after trying to fill with pencils. It will look better.

Before   After

Another exercise would be do a few solid lines of all tones. Then you grab the paper stump and pass over it, starting from the dark side of the pencil stroke and blend it over towards the lighter part. You will see this starting to build a nice dark to light shading effect. This way you will be getting familiar with the supplies.

Chapter 5

"Shadows and light"

Artistic Intelligence
"How to unlock the artist within"

So, keep in mind that the light is always on the opposite side from where the dark is. It is always a fold or bend that creates this. An example is when you are looking at a portrait, and you see that underneath the chin is dark and has a shadow. Then the chin is the curve that caused for a shadow to form. It is dark because it is in the opposite direction from the light. When you get some sunlight and you look back behind you, notice that you have a shadow. That is because your body is blocking light and does not allow the opposite side to receive light. It all depends where the light is hitting the image.

The dark or shadow is always in the opposite direction. There are times where the shadows are fuzzy or sharp. Sometimes, there are more than one direction the light is hitting, so it creates a few shadows. The more detail you observe and pay attention to, the more 3D your art will be. Take a few hours to the entire day or week, to just simply do observation. Ask yourself a lot of questions.

Some good questions would be "what pencil will help me get that tone?

What hand stroke will help me get that texture? What kind of edges does that shadow have?" The more questions you ask yourself about how you would master that detail, the more your mind will start capturing how to do the process. This is about training your mind to memorize tones and to mentally visualize yourself repeatedly approaching the drawing step by step. By the time you get to draw the actual image, you will be more mentally prepared to do so with more confidence.

So, let's meditate on the image and take notes. Now, I want you to make 7 copies of your chosen image. Copy number 1 will be used to teach you the first observation. Grab a pencil, pen or

53

marker for this exercise. I invite you to circle all the highlights of the image.

Copy number 1 will not be written on.

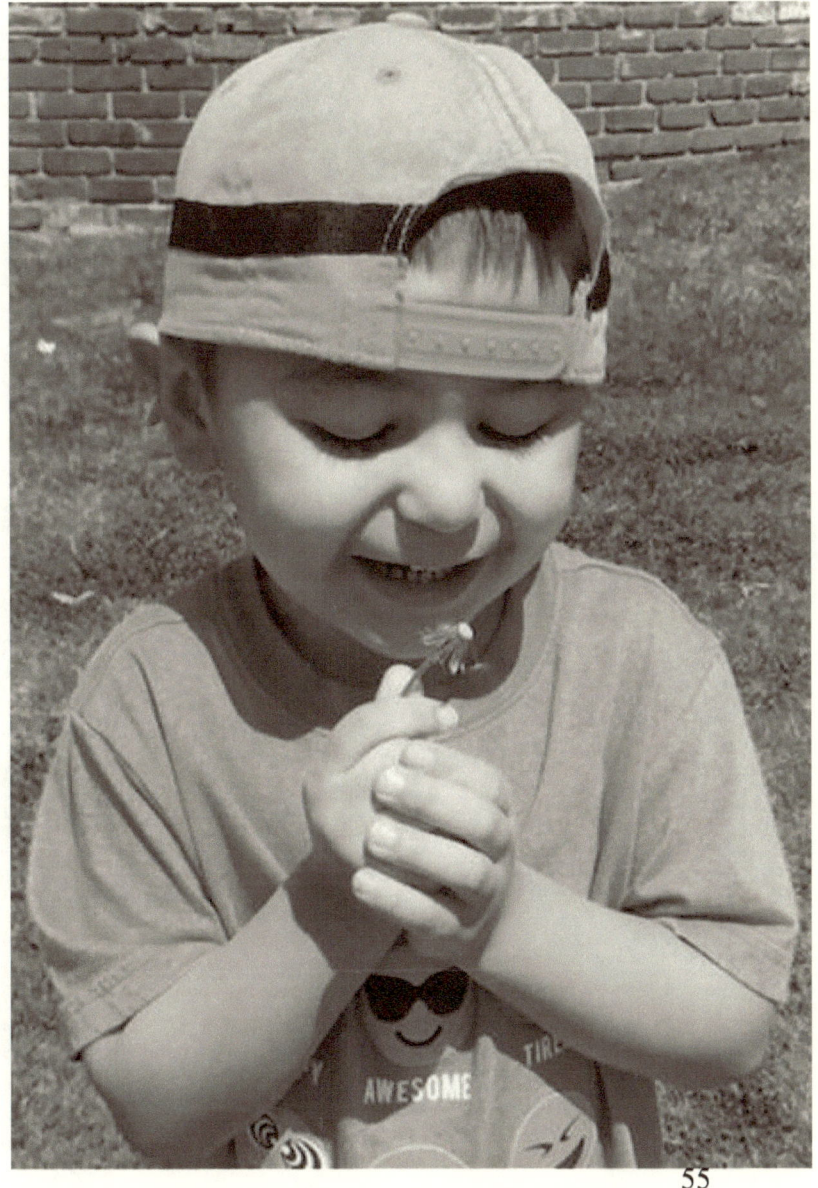

Grab copy number 2. Circle all the
brightest highlights. It should look like
this:

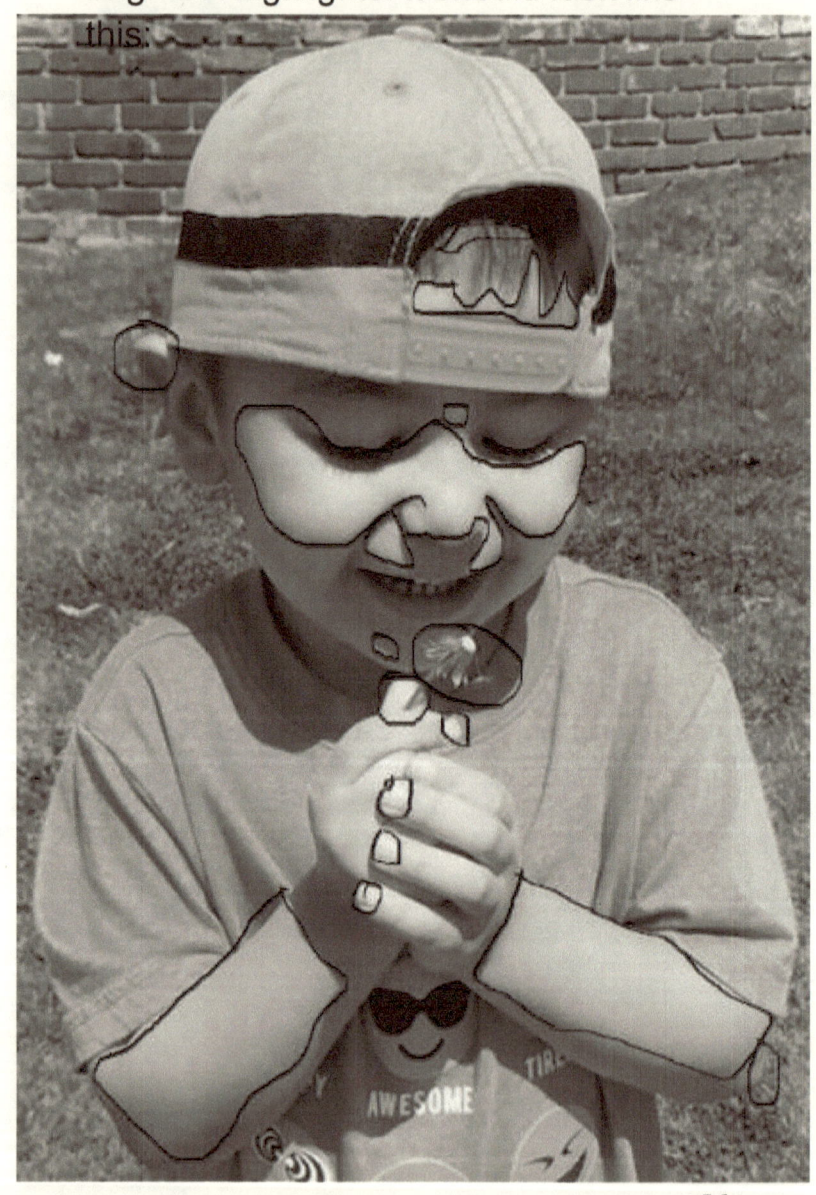

56

Now, in this exercise, I want you to grab copy number 3 and circle all the darkest parts of the image. Like this:

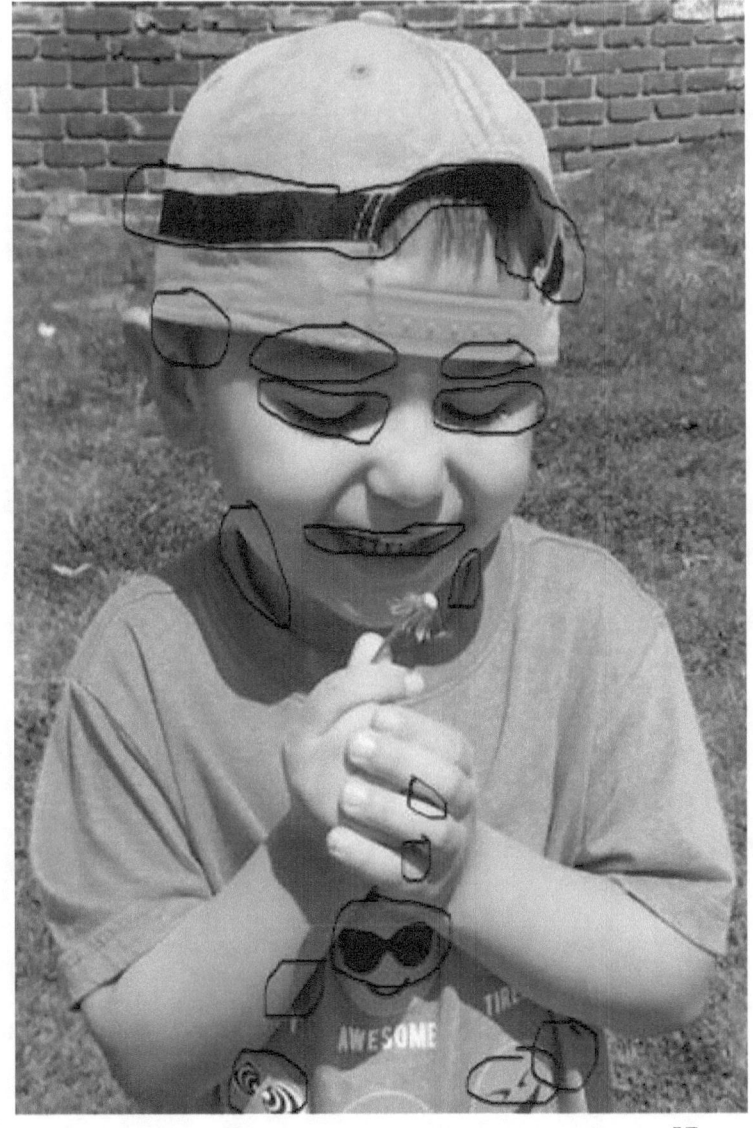

57

Grab copy number 4 and circle all the
middle tones of the image. Like this one:

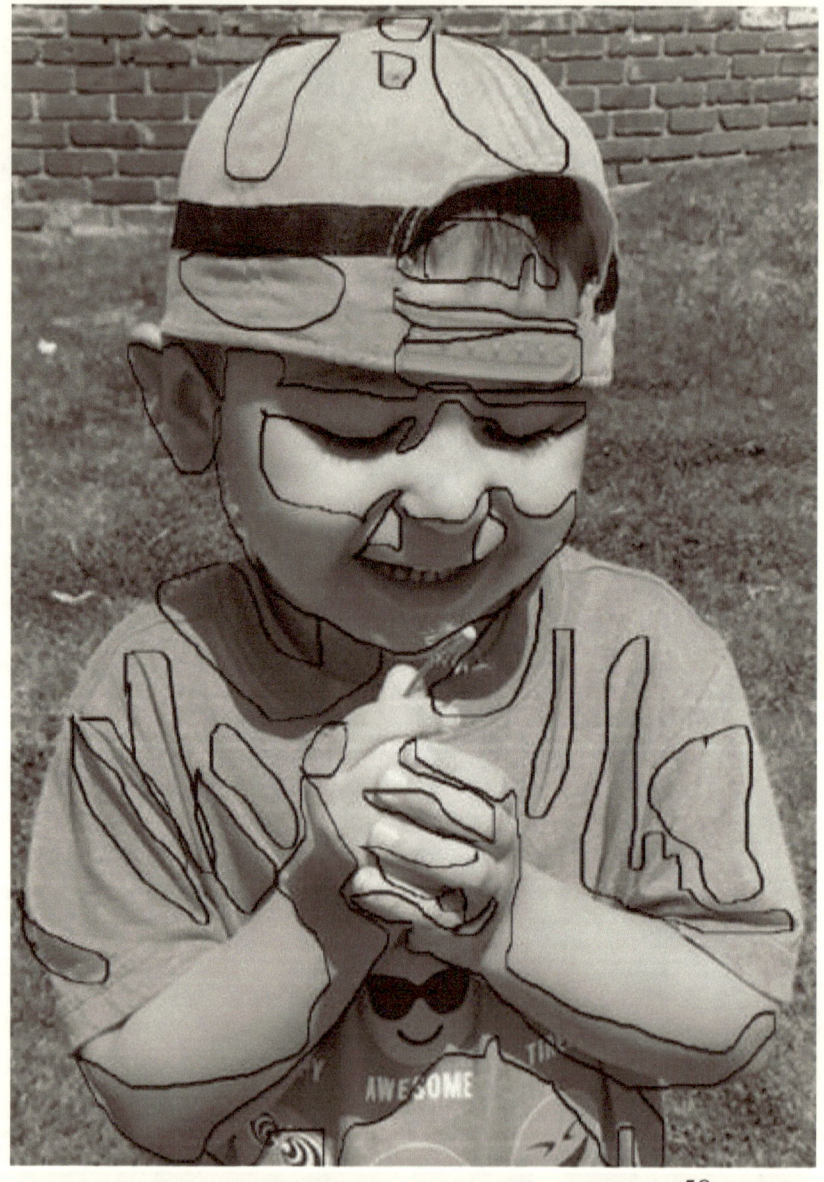

58

Grab copy number 5 and with pencil, pen or marker, try to label as best as possible. Label it with the grade scale pencil you use to accomplish on mimicking that image tone that you did using the miracle graph. The next pages will be shared examples.

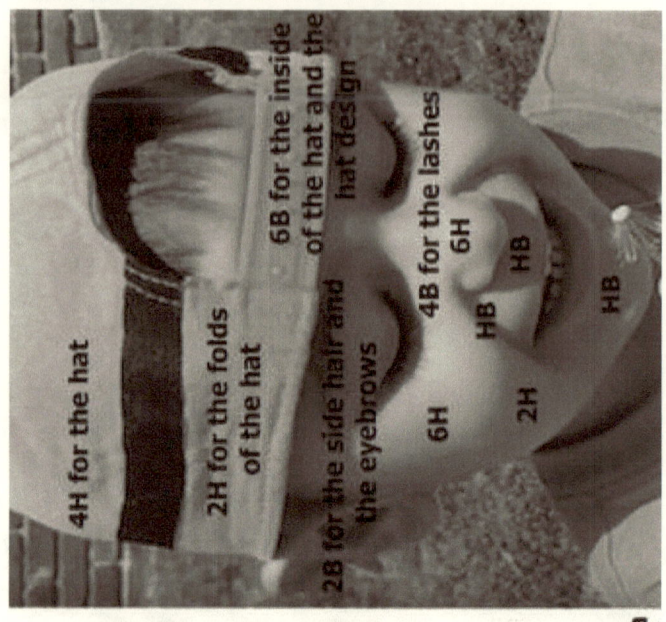

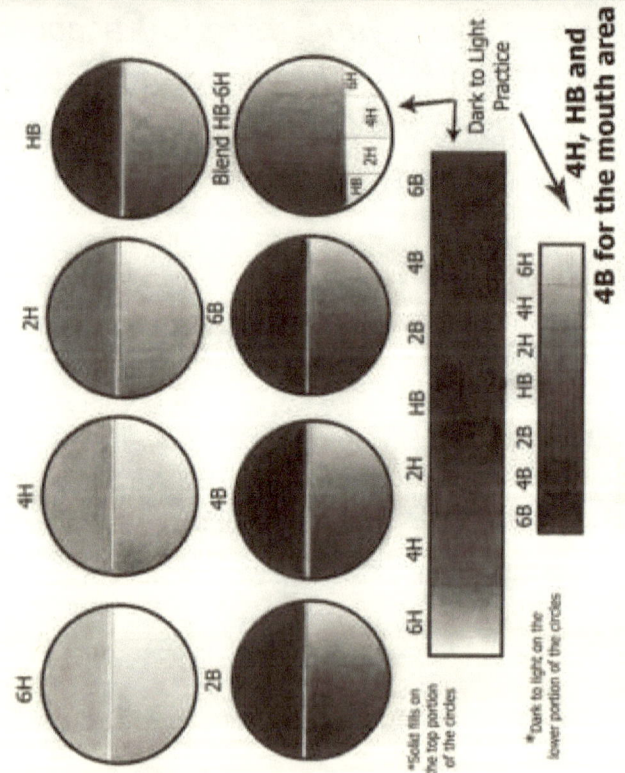

*Compare the image to the grey scale warm up exercise you did on the earlier chapter. Do you see how the scale is similar?

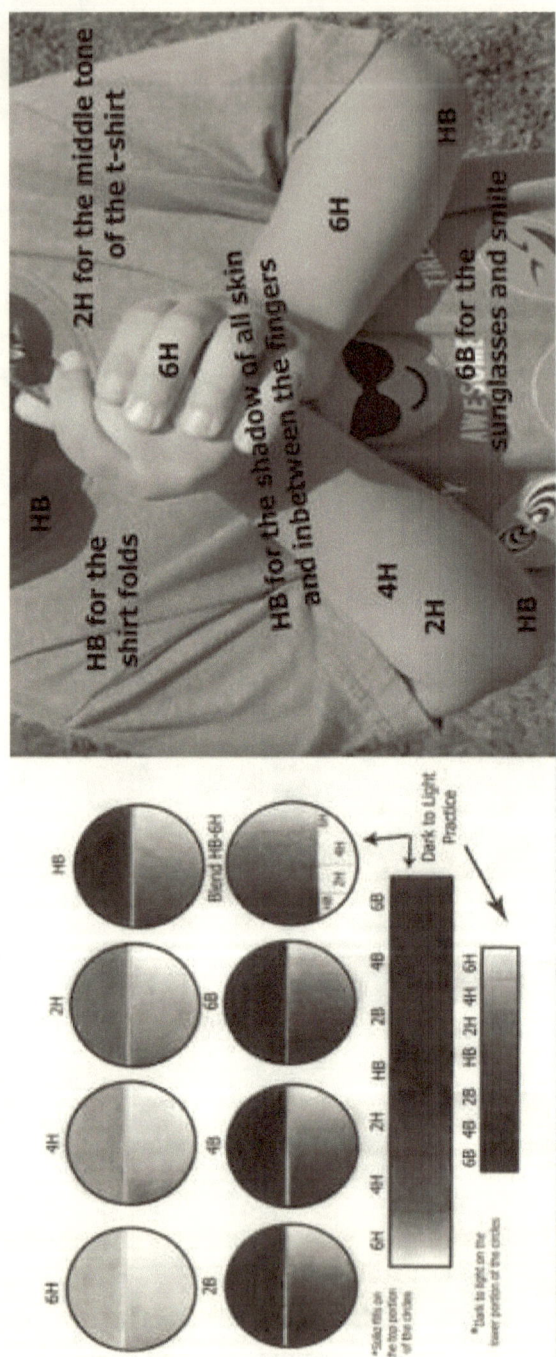

62

Once you get through all these exercises, you will be able to detect different tones, highlights, contrast and how to transfer the image. You will also already know what supplies to use.

Artistic Intelligence
"How to unlock the artist within"

Chapter 6

"Preparation and transferring"

Artistic Intelligence
"How to unlock the artist within"

.

Now, for the purpose of showing you how to shade, I invite you to trace the black and white image you chose. There are different ways to transfer the image. I will tell you a few and you can choose how you want to do it. You can use the graphite paper. This is very messy and if pressed too hard while tracing, the trace can be hard to erase and disappear with the blends. Put the blank paper on a solid table or board and add a very small piece of tape to at least two of the edges on the blank paper. This way it does not move while you are doing the tracing. Then you add the graphite paper on-top of the blank paper.

Make sure you put the graphite part facing the blank paper. You get copy number two and place it onto the graphite paper. Add a small piece of tape on the top of the chosen image and on just one side of the image. It would make it easier to see what is left when lifting the image. If you do it this way the image won't move, and you can feel free to lift and check as needed. I like to use a different colored pen when doing the tracing, so I can keep track of what I already went over. Use whatever makes it easier for you and just stay away from markers. This is about developing you and finding yourself as an artist. So, go ahead and trace everything as light as possible.

What makes it easier for me to determine what is what would be to add circles, lines, and "X's" throughout the image. That way you know what stays bright and empty or very lightly shaded. For the very dark areas, I can approach it a little heavier so that it is just a little bolder. The "X's" would be for the very darkest areas. That way I know those areas are the darkest part of the image. For the medium tones, some very light lines are good so that you know that the tone is in between.

69

You can also use a light box and trace with that by placing the image underneath. It is recommended for a darker setting in the room so that you can see the actual image through the blank paper. Always tape the back-ground image. The way I did it when I was very little since, we really didn't have much growing up was, I would tape the image and blank paper to my window! I'm not saying to do this! I am just sharing a piece of my childhood!

Trace the image with copy number 6. Here is an example of how one may look like. There is no right or wrong. Try your best and draw what you see, not what you think. When it comes to tracing,

70

it is how you feel you may accomplish finishing the image. As you notice, with the grey scale warm up exercise, you have already sketched those tones. You just need to train your mind on where to place them. Pay attention to the hard or soft edges. Here is an idea of how it would look after doing the tracing:

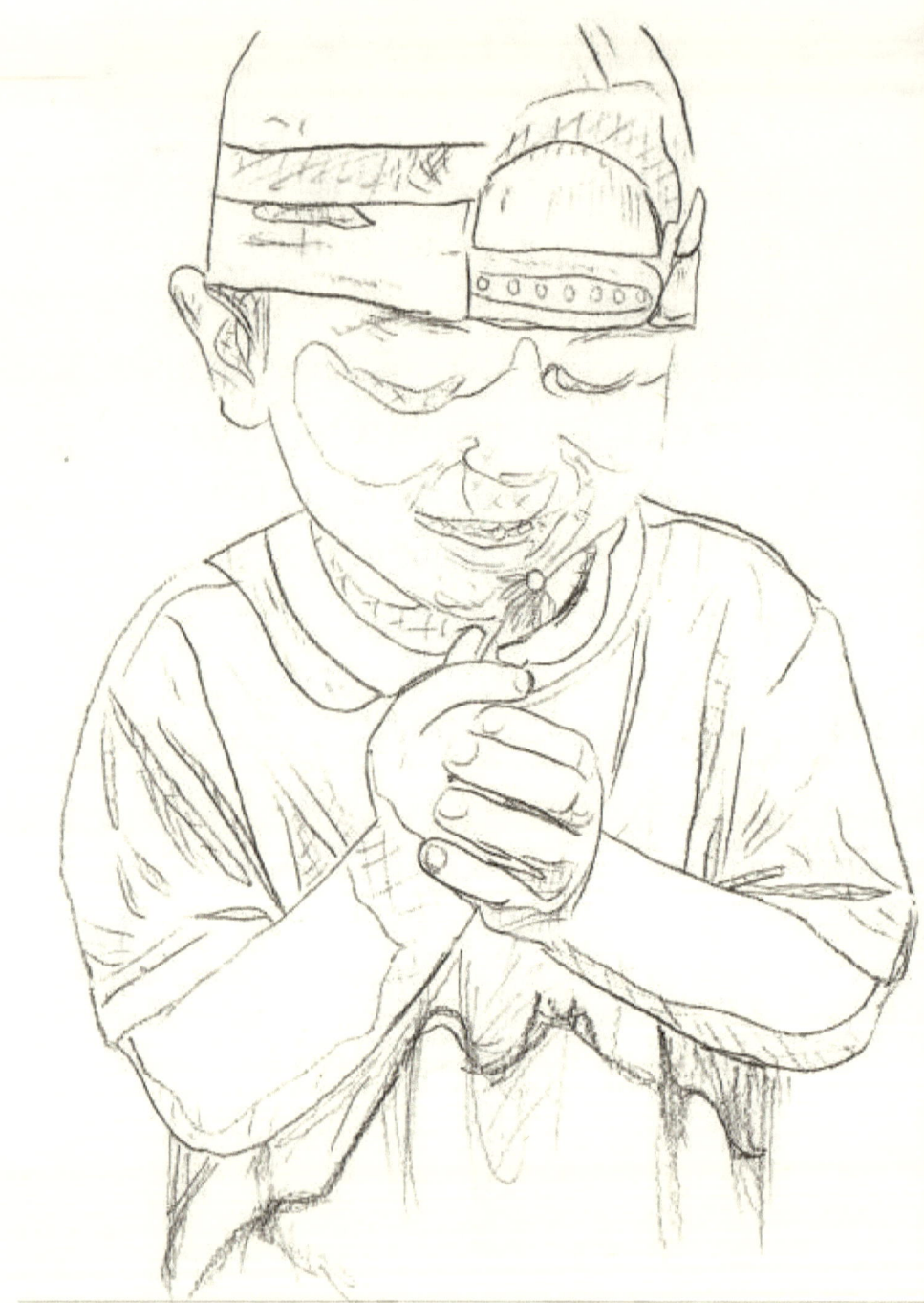

Chapter 7

"Put the shading to practice"

Artistic Intelligence
"How to unlock the artist within"

We can now talk about how to practice the actual shading using your chosen image. Okay, so first things first. One thing you need to keep in mind is that 3D has no outlines. Look around the room or the place you are in. Just meditate and do some observation. I'm sure you don't see any outlines, just objects, landscape or people. Great, so how do we create the same realism on paper? Simple, let's start digging in. First, you need to master shading and blending because it is from there that we can put what was taught into practice.

Try not to have a heavy hand or press too much on the paper. We do not want to create any dents. This will ruin the image especially if you need to erase or lighten up a section. All the dents will come out and destroy the quality. Don't forget to lighten your hand stroke as you get to a lighter shade.

The same copy you just traced on will be the image we will use to put it all together. I always recommend starting with the darkest areas, and then you move towards the middle tones. This way, from the middle tones you can fade them away to a lighter gradient, so that the highlight will come out on its own. You want to leave the highlight areas alone. They will slowly come out as you add more layers.

You do not have to make it look extremely dark on your first try. This is about having patience and building the look. Just make the marked areas that are marked to have the darkest gradient a little darker. Fill it in and map it out.

For the dark process, use the 4B to 6B pencils. After you darken the darkest areas, it will start looking like this:

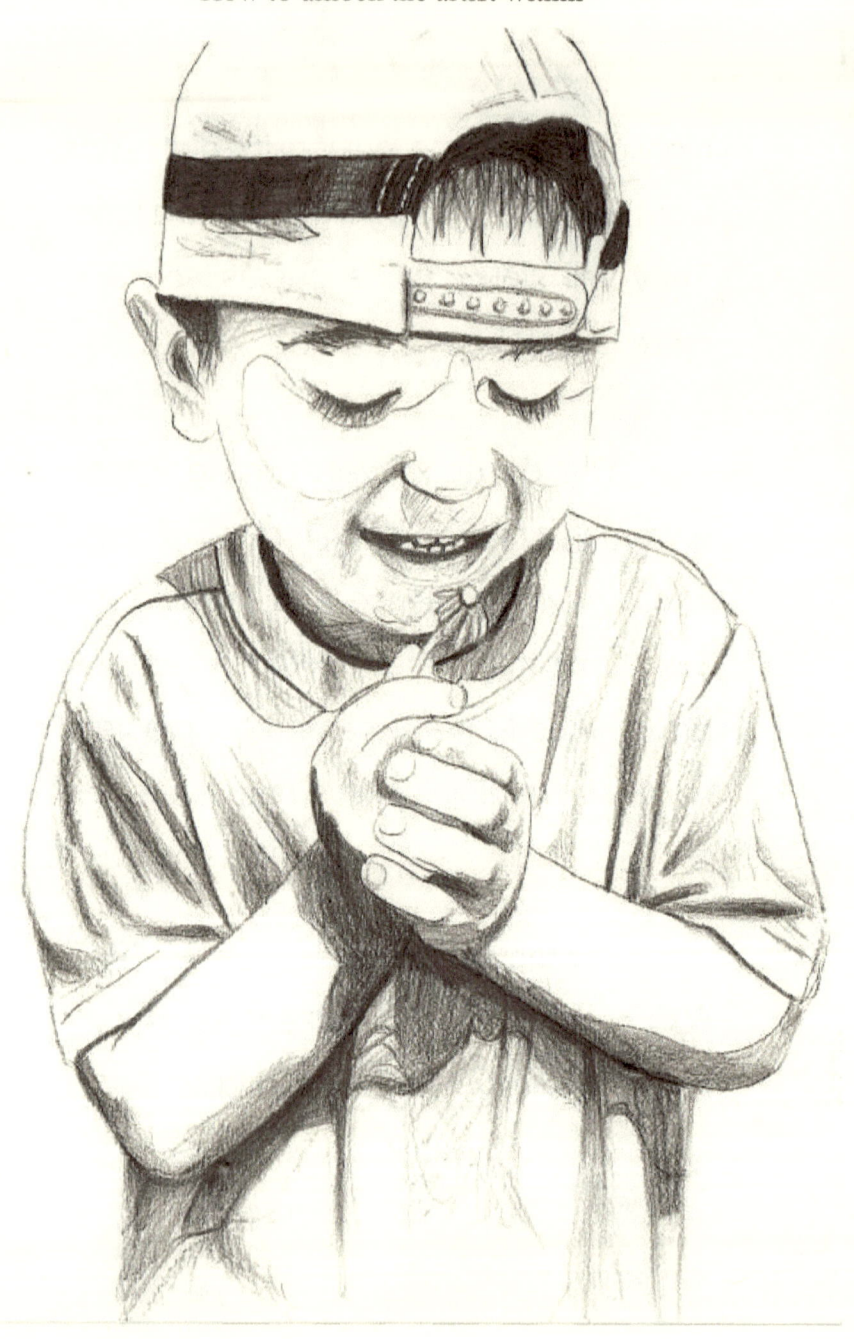

78

In between doing a solid pass. Sometimes it will have some inconsistence stroke marks. This is okay. Grab the paper stump and very lightly, pass right over all the dark areas as if you used a pencil again. Watch how it starts to blend in together. Then do the same process with the pencils to get a darker look. Repeat the pass with the stump again. Do this until you get the dark tone that you are looking for.

Once you finished with that, this is the time you will utilize all the other pencils. Pay attention to weather the shading and shadow is solid or soft. Go ahead and match the tones. It is easier to start from the dark and work your way towards all the lights. Follow the Miracle Shading graph.

Look at the copies of all the pictures, go through your notes. Using notes from labeling what pencil goes with what part of the skin tone, grab that actual pencil and start sketching in the area. I recommend always work your way from dark to light. Pencil as solid as you can and match tones. Then pass the paper stump. Repeat till you get the tone

you desire. Fade from dark to light. Keep
this in mind all the time.

Artistic Intelligence
"How to unlock the artist within"

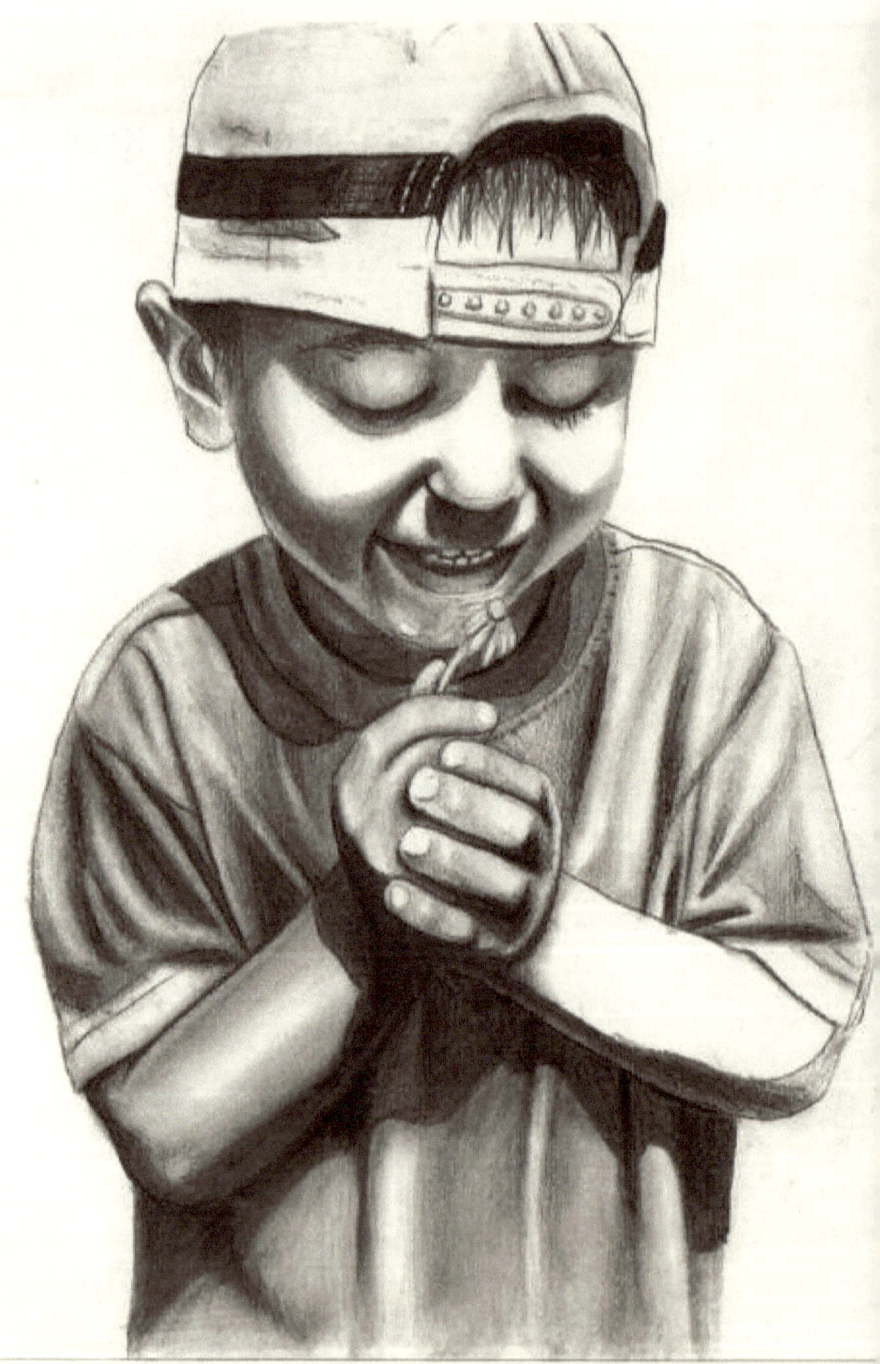

Fixing a quick mistake

As you can see, I over shaded the child's right arm. A good way to fix this would be to use the kneadable eraser. This eraser is great because by dabbing it a little, it can slightly start lighting up the over shaded areas. Try not to press too hard. The regular erasers will erase more than intended.

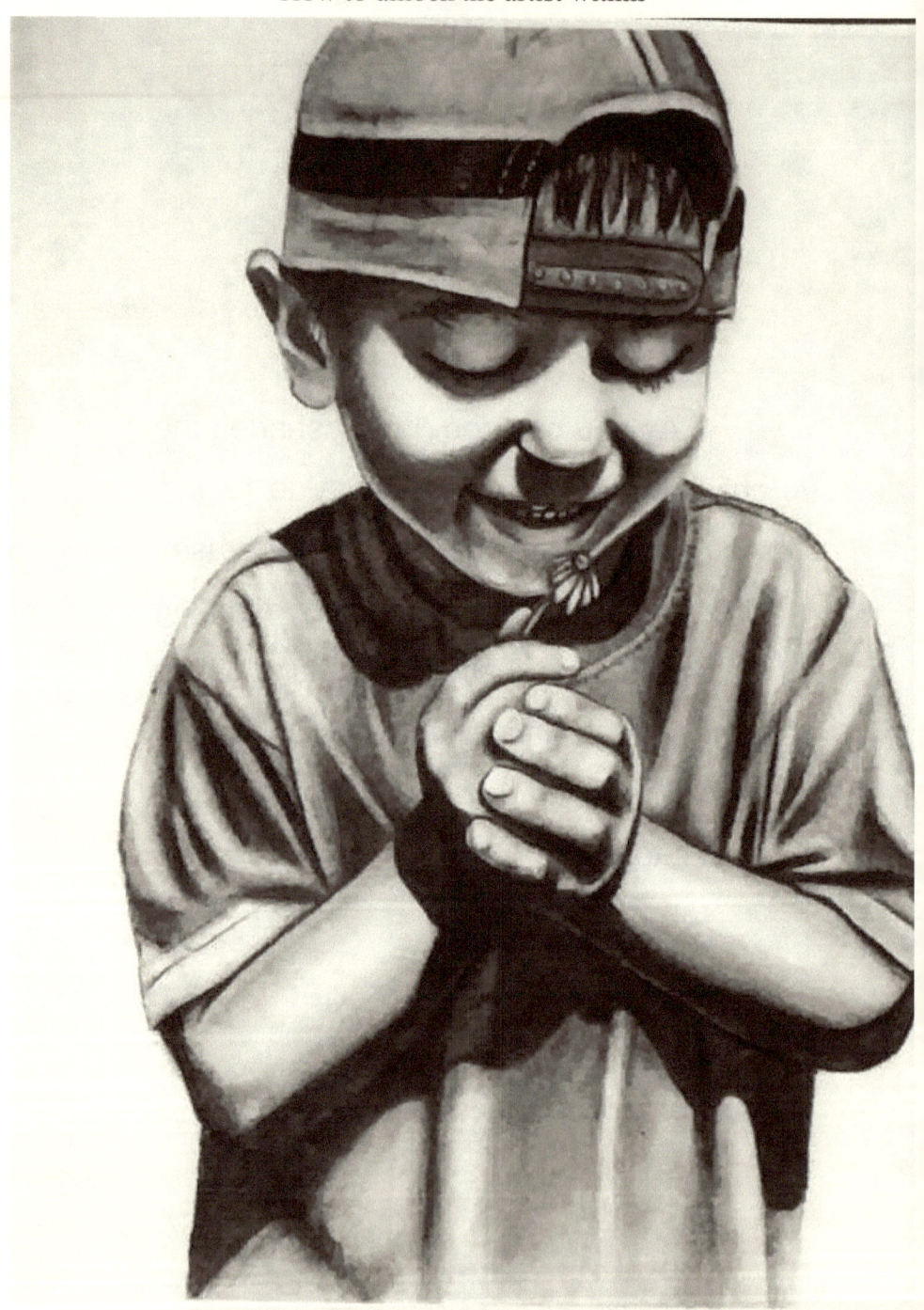

Chapter 8

"Review what you learned"

Artistic Intelligence
"How to unlock the artist within"

So now, you are a little bit familiar to:

- *Shading*

- *Blending*

- *Supplies*

- *Transferring the image*

- *Tracing the image*

- *Warm-ups and exercises*

- *Fixing a mistake*

- *Building a look*

- *How shading should not look like*

- *Highlights*

- *Contrast*

- *Shadows*

- *Middle tones*

- *The Miracle Graph*

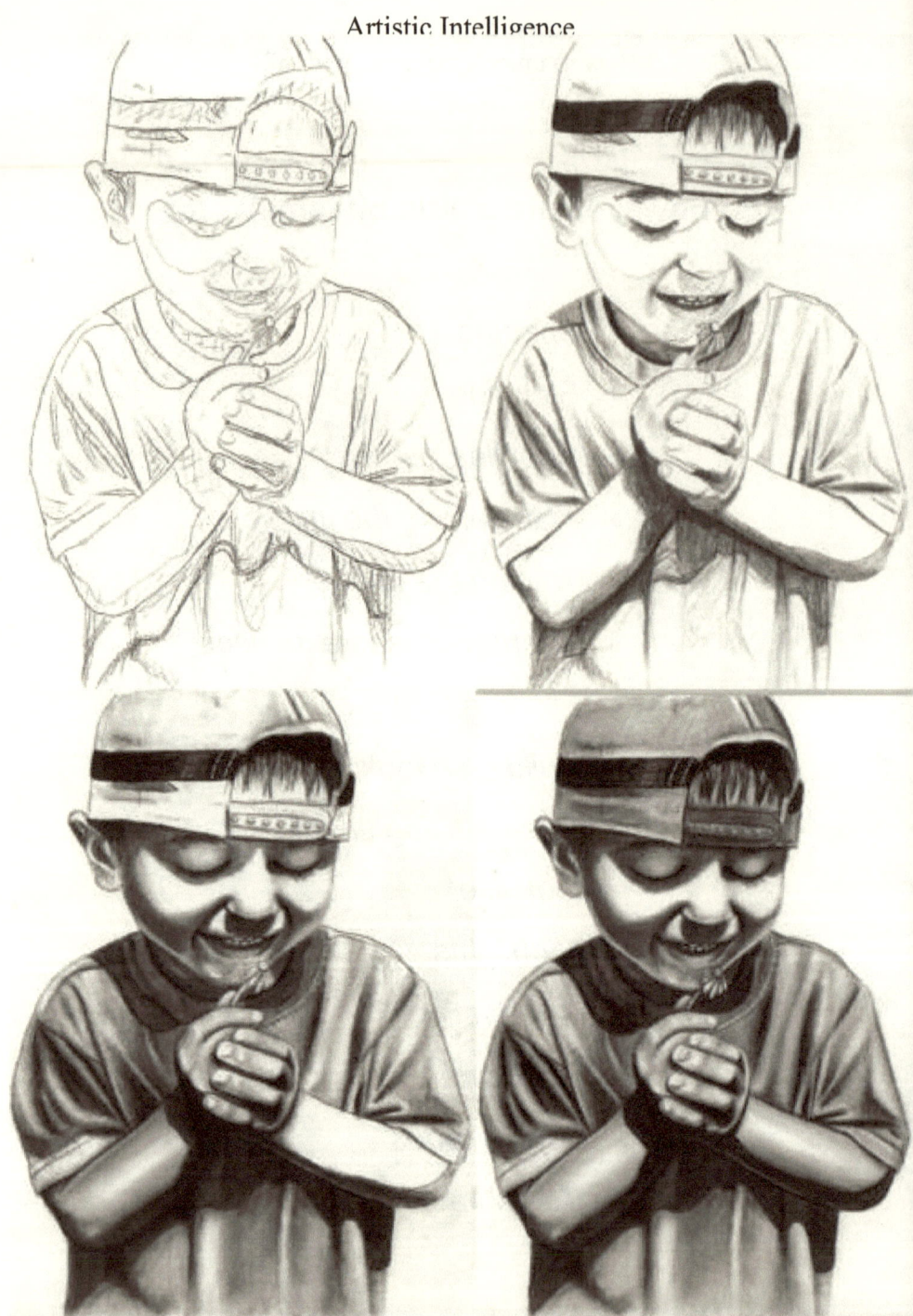

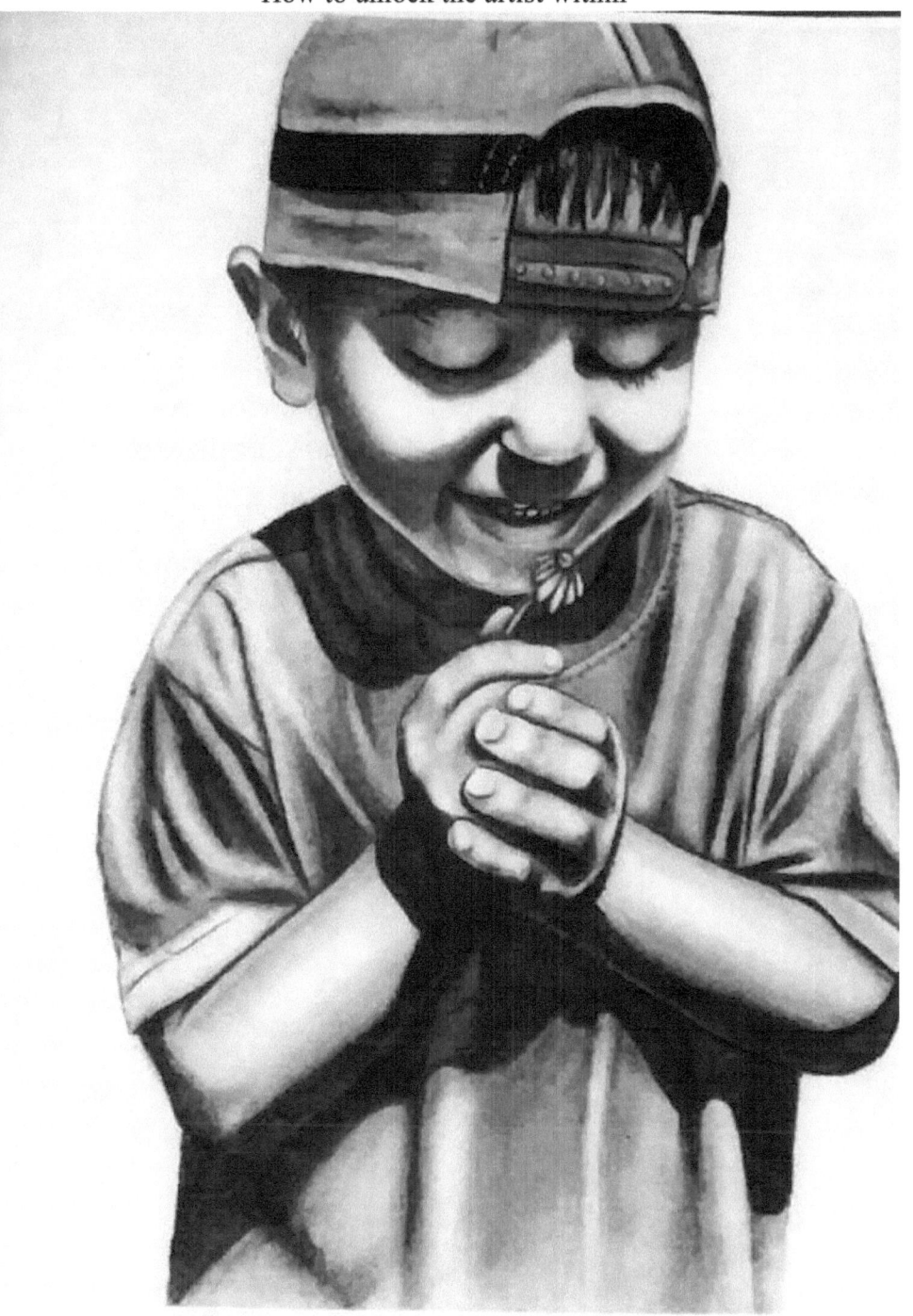

I enlarged the Miracle Graph so that you can make as many photocopies as you like. This way you can get straight to shading.

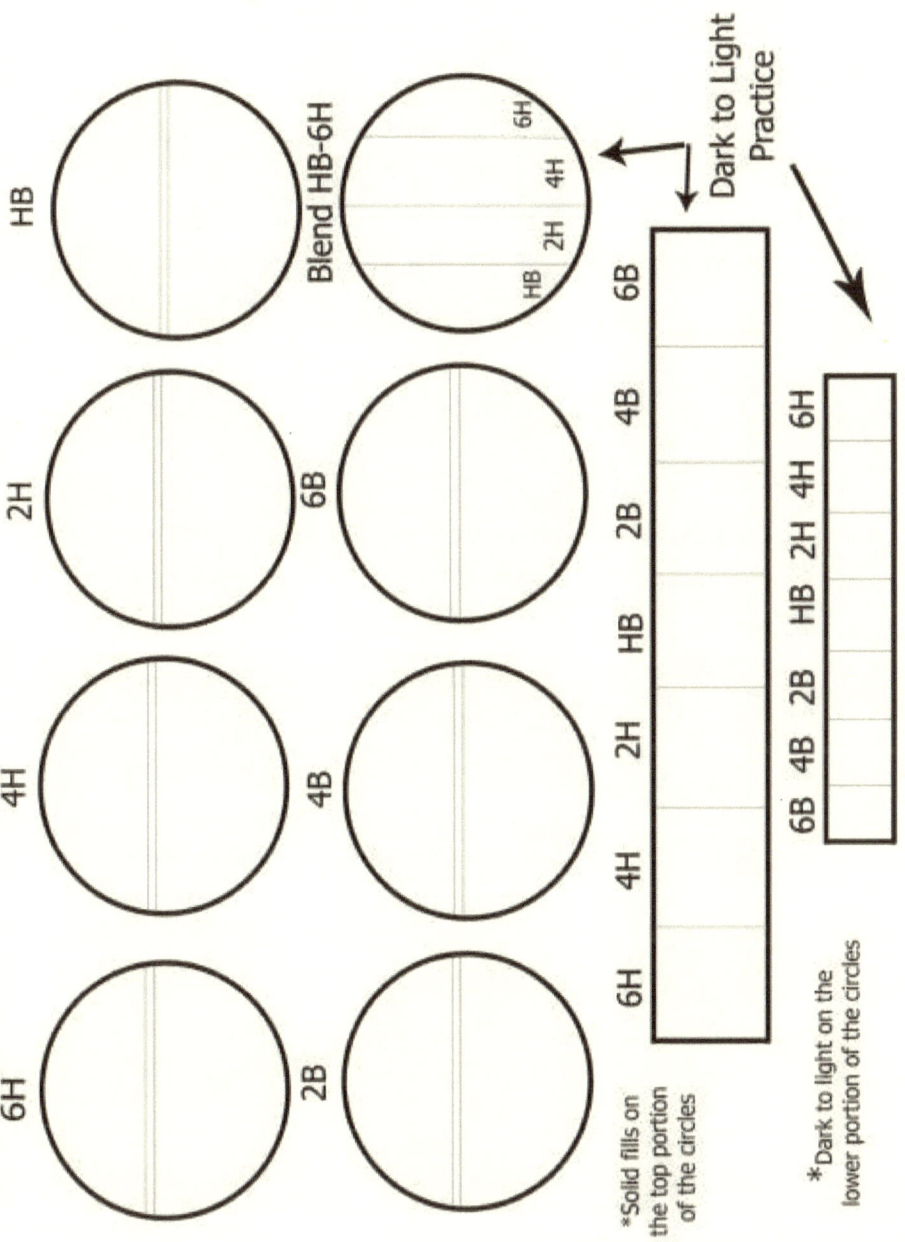

91

Artistic Intelligence
"How to unlock the artist within"

A message from the author…

For those who buy my book, I will give you one hour free of further explanation, feedback and support on your work with open questions and answers. We can get in touch via skype if it means to help you. To set up an appointment, reach me via email.

Please email me at:
Rebellious.spirit.59@gmail.com
Website:
www.rebellious-spirit59.com

Artistic Intelligence
"How to unlock the artist within"

You can find more books and audio books from the author Angelique Stefan on Amazon, Kindle, iTunes and Audible. Just type in her name on the search bar or go to her website!

Artistic Intelligence
"How to unlock the artist within"

Don't forget to watch the show called "Guess my hustle." The author was featured in an hour-long episode as a "tattoo and visual artist." She was fortunate to have this book featured in this show!

Artistic Intelligence
"How to unlock the artist within"

Acknowledgements

Artistic Intelligence
"How to unlock the artist within"

Being an artist is not always easy, there are a lot of issues that can get in your way. My friend Patrick Rodriguez has been my spiritual mentor for several years now. Him specializing in intuitive energy healing has really helped me accomplish my goals as an artist. I invite any and all people to allow someone like him to really help you meet your goals. It is not that you don't have it in you, it is trauma that does not let you see above the pain. A great way to understand all the things he can help you with is by going to his website or sending him an email.

Here are the services that he can provide to help you meet your life goals:

- *Healing with love*
- *Stuck energy cleansing*
- *Facilitating as an empath*
- *Soul fragmentation therapy*
- *Spirit release*
- *Chakra Balancing*
- *Hypnotherapy*
- *Theta healing*
- *Angel healing*

"Releasing your past, to open your present"

-Patrick Rodriguez

Website:

https://soulhealingtherapy.com/

Email:

patrick@patrickrodriguez.com

Notes: